I am 5!

WRITTEN BY
SHARI LAST

I am 5 and I listen to rock music.

I am 5 and I make a lot of mess.

I am 5 and I am very strong.

I am 5 and I go to the park every week.

I am 5 and I love taking selfies!

I am 5 and I love my pet.

I am 5 and I'm a bookworm.

I am 5 and when I grow up
I want to be a firefighter.

I am 5 and I love my family.

I am 5 and I love all vehicles!

I am 5 and I have my own diary.

I am 5 and I LOVE sparkly things!

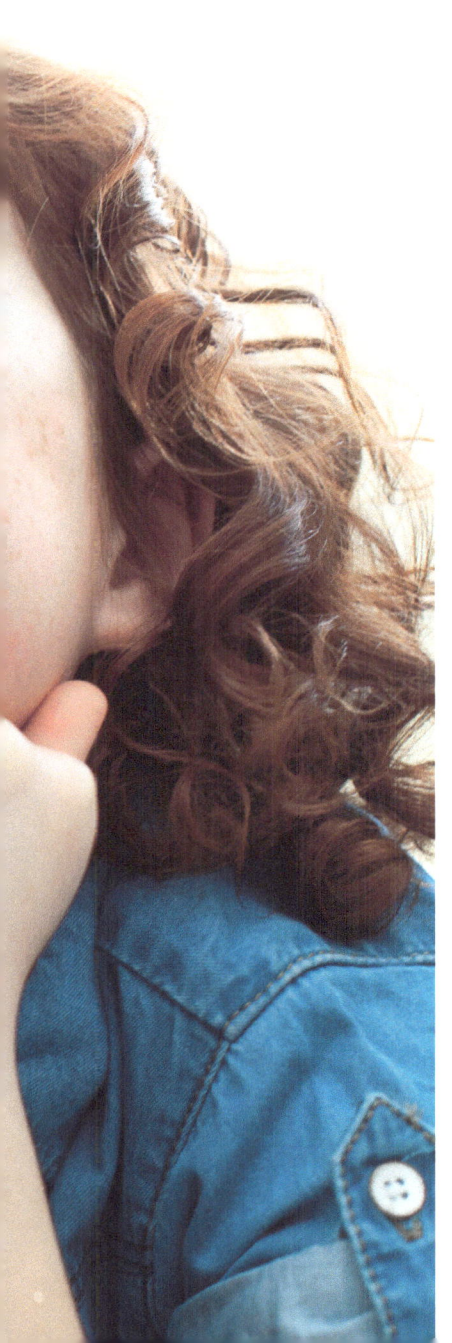

We are 5 and we play piano.

There is no ONE way to be 5.
There is no one way to be ANYTHING!

How would you describe yourself?

I am _____

I am _____

I am _____

Write down three things that make you YOU!

1.	2.	3.

First published in Great Britain in 2024
Cupcake Press,
an imprint of
TELL ME MORE Books

Text copyright ©2024 Shari Last
Design copyright ©2024 Shari Last

ISBN: 978-1-917200-10-3

Picture credits: Thanks to Adobe Stock.

All rights reserved. Without limiting the rights under the copyright reserved above, no part of this publication may be reproduced, stored in, or introduced into a retrieval system, or transmitted, in any form, or by any means (electronic, mechanical, photocopying, recording or otherwise), without the prior written permission of the copyright owner.

www.ingramcontent.com/pod-product-compliance
Lightning Source LLC
Chambersburg PA
CBHW050749110526
44591CB00002B/25